YOU CHO

DATE		
JUN 2 1 2014		
JUL 2 1 2014		
NO 0 3 '14		
11-7-14		

SO-BNT-252

You Choose Books are published by Capstone Press,
1710 Roe Crest Drive, North Mankato, Minnesota 56003
www.capstonepub.com

Library of Congress Cataloging-in-Publication Data
Hoena, B. A.
Hurricane Katrina : an interactive modern history adventure / by Blake Hoena.
pages cm. — (You choose. You choose: modern)
Includes bibliographical references and index.
Summary: "Describes the people and events involved during Hurricane Katrina in 2005.
The reader's choices reveal the historical details"—Provided by publisher.
ISBN 978-1-4765-4189-1 (library binding)
ISBN 978-1-4765-5220-0 (paperback)
ISBN 978-1-4765-6066-3 (eBook PDF)
1. Hurricane Katrina, 2005—Juvenile literature. 2. Hurricanes—Gulf States—Juvenile
literature. 3. Disaster victims—Gulf States—Juvenile literature. I. Title.
HV6362005.G85 H64 2014
976'.044—dc23   2013036666

Editorial Credits
Michelle Hasselius and Angie Kaelberer, editors; Gene Bentdahl, designer;
Wanda Winch, media researcher; Danielle Ceminsky, production specialist

Our very special thanks to the Louisiana State Museum for their curatorial review.

Photo Credits
AP Images: Dave Martin, 27, 45, Eric Gay, 62, Joe Holloway Jr., 74, John Bazemore,
80, 90, Phil Coale, 60, Rob Carr, 18, Robert Galbraith, 35, Vincent Laforet, cover;
Capstone, 9; Corbis: A.J. Sisco, 70, *Dallas Morning News*/Smiley N. Pool, 52, Reuters/
Richard Carson, 25, Reuters/Robert Galbraith, 64; FEMA News Photo: Jocelyn
Augustino, 31, 34, 42, 57, Mark Wolfe, 96, Marty Bahamonde, 20, 22; Getty Images
Inc: Barry Williams, 88, Bloomberg/Oscar Sosa, 98, Joe Raedle, 93, Marianne Todd,
95, Mario Tama, 67, Photo Researchers/Jim Reed Photography, 72, Science Faction/
Jim Reed Photography, 86, Time & Life Pictures/Lynn Pelham, 15; Newscom: Zuma
Press/Philippe de Poulpiquet, 47; NOAA, 6; Shutterstock: Andre Viegas, paper design,
Eric Isselée, 100, Laurie Barr, 12, 39, Nejron Photo, waves background, Tad Denson,
77, 83; U.S. Coast Guard Auxillary, National Department of Public Affairs, History
Division, 55

Printed in the United States of America in Stevens Point, Wisconsin.
092013   007765WZS14

TABLE OF CONTENTS

ABOUT YOUR ADVENTURE

YOU are living along the U.S. Gulf Coast in August 2005. A huge storm is headed your way—Hurricane Katrina. The Gulf Coast has withstood many hurricanes in the past. This time won't be any different—or will it?

In this book you'll explore how the choices people make can affect their lives and those of others. The events you'll experience happened to real people.

Chapter One sets the scene. Then you choose which path to read. Follow the directions at the bottom of each page. The choices you make will change your outcome. After you finish your path, go back and read the others for new perspectives and more adventures.

YOU CHOOSE the path
you take through history.

Hurricane Katrina is considered one of the worst natural disasters in U.S. history.

A Monster Storm

It is Wednesday morning, August 24, 2005. A tropical storm kicks up white-capped waves in the central Bahamas just Southwest of Florida. Winds whip around counterclockwise at nearly 40 miles per hour. Thunder rattles the sky. This tropical storm has all the makings of a hurricane. The National Hurricane Center names it Katrina. The next day Katrina's winds reach hurricane status. The storm barrels down on Florida.

Turn the page.

Katrina causes hundreds of millions of dollars in damages and several deaths in Florida. But it isn't finished yet.

Katrina crosses Florida's southern tip and enters the Gulf of Mexico. The Gulf's warm waters fuel the storm. Katrina quickly builds to a category 2 hurricane. It heads for the U.S. Gulf Coast.

As Katrina reaches category 3, the National Hurricane Center's forecast track shows it making landfall near New Orleans. The city of about 500,000 people is surrounded by water. It hugs the southern shore of Lake Pontchartrain. The Mississippi River winds through the city. Lake Borgne borders the city to the east. A marshy delta separates New Orleans from the Gulf of Mexico.

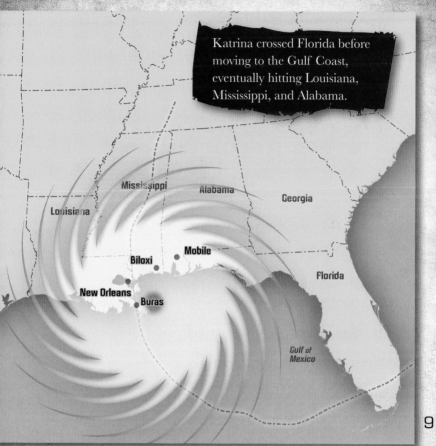

Katrina crossed Florida before moving to the Gulf Coast, eventually hitting Louisiana, Mississippi, and Alabama.

9

Governors Kathleen Blanco of Louisiana and Haley Barbour of Mississippi both declare states of emergency. National Guard and U.S. Coast Guard units are put on standby. Oil companies evacuate their rigs in the Gulf. State police are ordered to be on high alert. Many people living in threatened areas, including New Orleans, leave their homes and head to safety.

President George W. Bush declares a federal state of emergency Saturday, August 27. Federal agencies are now allowed to use their resources to help residents in the area. The Federal Emergency Management Agency (FEMA) prepares several teams. The agency also gathers supplies such as food, water, and blankets.

Early Sunday morning Katrina builds to a category 4 hurricane. Its storm surge—huge waves pushed to shore by the wind—could cause massive flooding. By 7:00 a.m., with winds topping 155 miles per hour, the hurricane reaches the rare category 5 status. Katrina is a monster storm.

You live along the Gulf Coast. What choices will you make with Hurricane Katrina barreling down on your home? Many of those choices will depend on where you live.

To be a child living in the Lower Ninth Ward of New Orleans, turn to page **13.**

To be a store owner in the Lakeview neighborhood in New Orleans, turn to page **43.**

To be a firefighter in Biloxi, Mississippi, turn to page **73.**

The Ninth Ward in New Orleans suffered extensive damage after the storm caused breaches in nearby canals.

CHAPTER 2

Survival in the Lower Ninth Ward

You're 10 years old and live with your family in the Lower Ninth Ward. This area of New Orleans is in the southeastern corner of the city. It runs up against St. Bernard Parish. The Mississippi River is just to the south, and the Industrial Canal borders it on the west.

Most of the houses in your neighborhood are small, single-story homes. Some are run down, but many, like your family's, are well kept. Your house contains everything you own, from your dog Zuki to your toys and clothes.

13

Turn the page.

You and your friends often run along the grassy side of the levees that separate your neighborhood from the city's canals. You have seen their waters rise and fall with the seasons. But never in your short lifetime have those barriers really been tested.

Hurricane Katrina is all over the news by Saturday, August 27. It's now a category 3 hurricane. The next morning you hear Mayor Ray Nagin on the radio. He orders a mandatory evacuation of New Orleans. This is the first time that this has ever happened. But like thousands of others in the city, your family can't afford to own a car. There isn't any free public transportation to take you out of the city. You have no way of leaving.

"We don't need to go anywhere," your mom says. "My parents rode out Hurricane Betsy back in 1965. Katrina can't be any worse than that. And everything we own is here. Someone might steal our things if we don't stay."

Your dad seems less sure. While you can't leave the city, you could go to a shelter. But that would mean leaving everything behind, even Zuki. Pets aren't allowed at the shelter.

Hurricane Betsy hit New Orleans on September 9, 1965.

To stay at home, turn to page **16**.
To go to the shelter, turn to page **20**.

"We can't leave Zuki!" you plead with your parents. Dad sighs and agrees with you and Mom.

While your dad boards up the windows of your house, you and your mom walk to K &M Super Market on the corner to pick up a few supplies.

On the way to the store, you see your friend Alisha. You ask if she is afraid.

"I've never been scared of a hurricane," she says. "It's just wind. And where could we go, anyway?"

The streets are nearly deserted, but the few people you see don't look scared. Some are proud to be staying. Others simply have nowhere else to go.

At the store Mom picks through the bare shelves and grabs a few bottles of water and spare batteries for your radio. Then you head back home.

That night thunder rumbles to the south. The wind picks up, and the rain begins. You fall asleep listening to the radio. "Katrina will weaken as it nears land but could come ashore as a category 4 hurricane …"

You start to worry. Most levees in the city are designed to resist the storm surge from a category 3 hurricane, but not a category 4. What will happen when Katrina makes landfall?

You sleep restlessly. Sometime after 7:00 a.m., your parents wake you. Everything is dark. There is no power and all the lights are out.

"We've been listening to the radio," Mom shouts over the roaring winds. "Katrina made landfall more than an hour ago."

"The streets are beginning to flood," Dad yells. "Water must be topping the levees."

Turn the page.

You run to the front stoop. Water covers the first step. Much of the Lower Ninth Ward is slightly below sea level. Once the area starts to flood, you could be in danger.

Some stores stayed open, even after the damage caused by Hurricane Katrina.

18

To move to the attic of your house, go to page **19**.

To leave before the water rises, turn to page **32**.

Your house has just one story, but it does have a small attic. Your dad pulls down the ladder leading to the attic. You help your parents carry food, water, and clothes into the attic.

As you are working, a wall of water rushes by outside. Water leaks through the windows and seeps under the door of your house. Water from Katrina's storm surge is being forced into the Intracoastal Waterway and the Industrial Canal. That water must have caused one of the levees to give way.

The water inside your house keeps rising. Now you really are scared.

To get into the attic, turn to page **30.**
To leave your home, turn to page **32.**

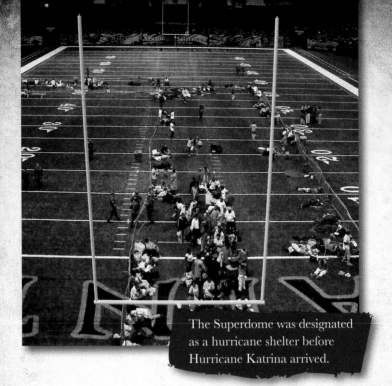

The Superdome was designated as a hurricane shelter before Hurricane Katrina arrived.

Your dad convinces your mom that you should seek shelter at the Superdome. It's the arena where the New Orleans Saints football team plays. Some people say the building can withstand winds of up to 200 miles per hour.

"We should be safe there," Dad says.

"But what about our things?" Mom asks.

"We can always buy new things," he sighs.

Mayor Nagin says on the radio to bring pillows and blankets. Your parents also gather clothes and bottled water, plus a few family photos. But your dog has to stay. You cry as you say good-bye to Zuki. You leave food and water for her, but you don't know if you'll ever see her again.

You walk to the nearest pickup station and join a line of other people going to the Superdome. You wait hours in the heat for a bus as dark clouds loom overhead. When your bus reaches the Superdome, people are being searched for weapons before being allowed inside. You again wait in line for several hours.

Turn the page.

The Superdome is a huge structure, standing 273 feet tall. Its dome is 680 feet in diameter. During football games the stadium holds more than 70,000 people. You file inside with about 10,000 other people. Volunteers lead your family to a group of seats where you will stay.

As the day wears on, you hear the winds picking up outside. Rain beats down on the dome. The people next to you have a battery-operated radio.

Residents brought their belongings and waited in lines for hours to get into the Superdome.

You are lulled to sleep by the weather reports. "It's expected that Katrina will weaken to a category 4 hurricane as it comes ashore …"

Just after 5:00 a.m. everything goes dark. The Superdome loses power. Backup generators kick in, but they have only emergency lighting. The air conditioning is off.

You try to go back to sleep. But about three hours later you hear a loud groan from above. You look up and watch in horror as the wind tears away a 15-foot section of the roof. Water pours onto the field. Then another section of roof is torn away. The building creaks and moans. You hear your parents whispering.

23

"I don't know if the dome's strong enough," Mom says.

"Should we leave?" Dad asks.

To stay, turn to page **24.**

To leave, turn page **27.**

You speak up. "Mom, it's scary here, but it's going to be worse outside."

"We're here now—we might as well stay," Mom says. "Let's not risk going outside with the hurricane blowing past."

Later that morning you and Mom stand in line for food. A member of the National Guard hands you an MRE, a military food ration, and a bottle of water. When you get back to your seat, your dad shows you how to heat the MRE. You get sloppy joes with tortillas and orange drink mix. There are also cookies and chewing gum. It almost feels like you are camping.

When you are not standing in line for food, you hover near the people with the radio to listen to the news. "The Lower Ninth Ward has been submerged …"

"We're lucky we left," Mom says.

But you aren't so sure. As the day wears on, toilets back up and sewage covers the floors. Trash begins to pile up. People whisper rumors about people who have been beat up or even killed at the dome. You even think you hear a gunshot.

The Astrodome in Houston was also used by residents to ride out the storm.

Turn the page.

During the next two days, conditions worsen at the Superdome. More people arrive. They are survivors that rescue teams either pulled from the roofs of their homes or found stranded along overpasses. Sometimes you have to wait half a day for more food to arrive. And you don't dare go to the bathrooms any more. They are dirty, smelly, and dark. Instead you find a spot outside.

People are saying that FEMA buses are on the way to take everyone to Houston, Texas. But no one knows when or if they will arrive.

To leave the Superdome, turn to page **37.**
To wait for the buses, turn to page **40.**

More sections of the roof rip away. As more water pours in, panic increases. Some people cry in fear as they gather up their belongings and move away from the spots where water is coming in. Others question whether the Superdome will be strong enough to survive the storm. Some people are talking about going to the nearby Ernest N. Morial Convention Center. You and your parents decide to leave.

High winds and rain damaged the Superdome's roof and caused it to leak.

Turn the page.

"Maybe things will be better at the convention center," you say hopefully. Your family quietly sneaks past the security guards.

Outside the storm is raging. Stinging rain beats down on you as you lean into the gusting winds. You are following your parents across the parking lot when Dad suddenly stops in his tracks. He clutches his chest.

"Dad, what's wrong?" you yell into the wind.

"Can't … breathe …," Dad manages to gasp before he collapses to the ground. Mom kneels down beside him. "Run back into the dome and get help!" she shouts at you as she checks Dad's neck for a pulse. "Hurry!"

You run back to the Superdome as fast as the rain and wind will allow.

As you burst through the doors, you see a security guard. "Come with me!" you plead. "My dad needs help!" Minutes pass while the guard tries to find a medic or nurse to help. When you, the guard, and the medic finally reach the parking lot, you see Dad lying on the ground, his eyes closed. Mom is next to him, sobbing. "It's too late," she cries. "He's gone!"

Your eyes sting with tears as you stare in disbelief at your mom. If only you had stayed in the dome, someone might have been close enough to help your dad. Even if you and your mom make it out of the Superdome, your life will never be the same.

THE END

To follow another path, turn to page 11.
To read the conclusion, turn to page 101.

"Let's get to the attic," you shout to your parents. At the top of the ladder, you look back to see if Zuki is following, but she's nowhere to be seen. While you call for your dog, you watch in horror as the water quickly creeps up the steps.

"I don't know if it's going to stop," you cry.

Mom is frantic. She grabs her cell phone and dials 9-1-1. No answer. She tries several more times. Nothing.

"Come on, answer!" she yells.

Dad rummages around the attic looking for a hammer or an ax—anything to punch a hole in the roof and escape. Then he starts pounding on the attic ceiling with his fists. But the boards won't give.

The Lower Ninth Ward was completely flooded after the breaks in the levees.

The water is now in the attic. It reaches your ankles, your knees, and then your waist, with no sign of stopping.

You stand and your parents crouch in the highest part of the attic. You try to raise your face above the water to suck air into your mouth. But the water keeps rising.

In some parts of the Lower Ninth Ward, the storm surge covers the neighborhood in more than 15 feet of water. That's just above the height of your house. You and your parents drown in your own attic.

THE END

To follow another path, turn to page 11.
To read the conclusion, turn to page 101.

"We better get out and find higher ground," Dad says. "Come on!"

You follow your dad. You grab the back of his shirt as he works his way through the front door. The water is already up to his chest and still rising. You are lifted off your feet as you kick forward. Your mother is right behind you.

"Where's Zuki?" you yell to her.

"I'm not sure, honey," she replies. "We can't worry about her now."

You can only hope that your dog is safe. With the rising water, you don't have time to go back into the house and look for her.

As you swim out into the street, a neighbor waves to you.

"Over here!" he shouts.

"Hey, it's Larry," your dad cries.

You all swim over to Larry. He holds a heavy punching bag in front of him. He's using it as a float.

"Grab on," he says. "I'll take you to a safe place."

Larry leads you to one of the two-story houses in the neighborhood. The owners, Mike and Kim, hang out one of the windows and pull you inside. Larry's sister, Joanna, is there with her three kids.

Once your parents join you, Kim says, "We have food and water. Whatever we have is yours." You're just thankful to be out of the wind and rain. But within a few hours, the temperature rises to 90 degrees. It is stifling inside. Between the heat and your limited supply of food and water, you know you can't stay here too long.

33

Turn the page.

"Maybe we can find a boat or something to get to higher ground," Mike suggests.

Your dad agrees. He and Mike head outside. The green water is now too deep to walk, so they swim down the street.

When they return about an hour later, they tow a small boat behind them. You and the other kids climb into it. Mike and your dad paddle it down the flooded street. The other adults swim alongside the boat as best they can.

Some survivors tried traveling in small boats to get through the flooded streets in New Orleans.

Thousands of people displaced by Hurricane Katrina waited for buses out of New Orleans.

Your group manages to cross the St. Claude Avenue Bridge into the Upper Ninth Ward, where the flooding isn't as severe. You seek shelter in the Frederick Douglass High School. You stay there for a day before heading to the Ernest N. Morial Convention Center, another makeshift shelter for storm victims. There you join thousands of hungry and thirsty people waiting for a bus to take them out of the city.

Turn the page.

You wait three days before boarding a bus headed to a shelter in Washington, D.C. It will be weeks or even months before you're able to return home, if you go back at all. You and your parents like living in the nation's capital. Maybe it will be your new home. You only wish you knew what happened to Zuki. You hope that she found safety with another family.

THE END

To follow another path, turn to page 11.
To read the conclusion, turn to page 101.

You and your parents have had enough. There are rumors of assaults and murders in the Superdome. The place is filthy and reeking of raw sewage. You don't feel safe. You aren't supposed to leave because the city is still flooded. But that night you sneak by the security guards.

"Where are we going to go?" you ask your parents. Dad shakes his head. "There's no way we can get home," he says. "But people are saying that the French Quarter wasn't hit too hard. That's where my boss, Mrs. Wright, lives. It's not too far to her house. Even if she evacuated, we can rest there a while until we figure out what to do." 37

Turn the page.

When you reach Mrs. Wright's house, she isn't there. But Dad finds a spare key under a mat on her front porch. He unlocks the door, and you all go inside. There's no electricity, but there's bottled water and canned food in the pantry. You stay there for five days, listening to news reports on a battery-operated radio.

Months later when you are finally allowed to return, you walk through the damaged streets back to the Lower Ninth Ward. Tears fill your eyes as you look at what's left of your house.

Before Katrina about 15,000 people lived in your neighborhood. It will be years before the cleanup is complete.

A home in the Lower Ninth Ward, one year after Hurricane Katrina

Then you hear barking. It's Zuki! She runs up to you and licks your face. The nub of her tail wags excitedly. You don't know how she survived. She is thin, dirty, and stinky. But at least she is one thing that you haven't lost in the storm.

THE END

To follow another path, turn to page 11.
To read the conclusion, turn to page 101.

With the Lower Ninth Ward flooded, you really have nowhere else to go. So you wait. Trash piles up. It is sweltering inside. And even though you are allowed to go outside, it's not much better there with all the people, the garbage, and the heat.

When the buses finally arrive September 2, you are happy to leave. You ride the bus to Houston's Astrodome, another shelter. You don't know how long you will be there. You don't know when you will return home—if ever. But at least you have food and a place to stay.

As you enter the Astrodome, you hear someone call your name. You turn and are surprised to see Alisha, your friend from the Lower Ninth.

"I can't believe we both ended up here!" Alisha says excitedly, throwing her arms around you.

"I'm so glad you're OK," you reply as you hug her back.

While you are in a strange place, at least you have a friend with you. After all you've lost, you are grateful for that.

THE END

To follow another path, turn to page 11.
To read the conclusion, turn to page 101.

Poor construction and design caused levees to fail, allowing Hurricane Katrina to flood 80 percent of New Orleans.

CHAPTER 3

To Stay or to Go: Lake Pontchartrain

You live in the Lakeview neighborhood of New Orleans. It is in the northwest corner of the city. Your neighborhood is tucked between the 17th Street and Orleans Avenue canals. Lake Pontchartrain is about a dozen blocks north.

During the days before Katrina's landfall, there are various reports about where it will strike. When the storm enters the Gulf of Mexico early Friday, August 26, forecasters say the storm is heading to the panhandle of Florida. But the forecast track shifts westward during the day. By that evening the track shows the center of the storm moving toward the Mississippi Gulf Coast. As Katrina moves across the Gulf, things look scarier for New Orleans.

43

Turn the page.

By Saturday the storm is headed straight for New Orleans, although forecasters say slight shifts are possible.

That afternoon Mayor Ray Nagin asks for a voluntary evacuation of the city. Thousands decide to leave. But you are not sure whether you should.

Two things make your decision difficult. You run a small neighborhood grocery store. Every day your store is closed, you lose money. And if you close, your customers may not be able to get needed supplies. Plus, your grandmother lives along the 17th Street Canal. She uses an oxygen tank to help her breathe, so it would be hard on her to leave. Either you or another family member will need to take care of her.

Highways out of New Orleans were packed with people trying to head inland to higher ground.

45

Turn the page.

On Sunday morning Mayor Nagin finally orders a mandatory evacuation of New Orleans. Landfall is expected in about 20 hours. You must decide what to do.

To stay with your grandmother, go to page **47**.

To leave town, turn to page **48**.

Many businesses in New Orleans were damaged or destroyed by Hurricane Katrina.

After closing your store Sunday night, you plan to go to your grandmother's. She owns a two-story house next to the 17th Street Canal. It's just blocks away from Lake Pontchartrain. You can take supplies over to her house and stay there. Or you can bring her back to your single-story grocery store.

To stay at your grandmother's, turn to page **54.**

To stay at your store, turn to page **58.**

You call your sister, Lori, to tell her of your plans. She is going to stay in the city and agrees to help your grandmother.

You board up your house and store. Once your car is packed, you drive to the nearest gas station. The Gulf produces about one-fourth of all U.S. oil and natural gas. You're surprised that station after station is closed and out of gas.

The gas station you finally find still open has a line of cars several blocks long.

To stay and fill up, go to page **49**.
To leave without filling up, turn to page **66**.

The day slowly wears on as you wait several hours to fill your gas tank. Then you take Interstate 10 west out of town. All lanes of the highway are open for outgoing traffic. But cars are still backed up for miles. You are just one of more than 1 million people who are evacuating the Gulf Coast because of Katrina.

You are thankful you filled your car's gas tank. Because of the traffic, it's several hours before you get out of the city.

You see cars stopped along the highway, packed with people and belongings. You hope that help comes soon so that the people are able to get to safety.

Turn the page.

As you drive, you listen to the weather reports. There is talk of a 17-foot storm surge pushing water through the city's canals. Most levees are 13 to 18 feet high, so there will be flooding. At least the levee walls should hold back most of the water.

That night you stay at your friend Jenny's house in Lafayette, about 135 miles east of New Orleans. Lori calls and says she took your grandmother to the shelter in the Superdome near downtown New Orleans. They should be protected from the storm there.

You stay up all night listening to the weather reports. At 6:10 a.m. Monday, Katrina makes landfall. As the minutes tick by, you hear of flooding in St. Bernard Parish and eastern New Orleans. Those sections of the city are far from your neighborhood. But the news isn't too bad. There has been damage, but nothing as serious as predicted.

Later that morning you fall asleep, thinking everything will be fine back home. You are tired from the trip yesterday and sleep through the night. When you wake up early Tuesday, you feel relieved about your city.

51

But as you listen to further reports throughout the day, your feelings change. There are breaches along the canals that drain into Lake Pontchartrain, including the 17th Street Canal.

Turn the page.

A breach in the 17th Street Canal caused massive flooding and damage to a large part of the city.

Your neighborhood is flooded, along with 80 percent of the city. More than 200,000 homes have been destroyed. Thousands of people are trapped in their homes, waiting for rescue workers to help them.

The next day you hear of widespread looting and shootings in New Orleans. There are rumors of murders and assaults at the Superdome. You worry about Nana and Lori. But you have no way to contact them. Cell phone service has been knocked out by the storm.

"I've got to go home," you tell Jenny. "I have to find Nana and Lori."

Jenny tries to talk you out of it. "You should stay here where it's safe. Someone will contact you about your family when phone service is restored."

To stay in Lafayette, turn to page **68.**
To leave Lafayette, turn to page **69.**

You pack your car with food, water, and extra emergency supplies, such as batteries and blankets. Then you drive to your grandmother's house. She smiles as you walk in carrying a box of supplies.

"I rode out Hurricane Betsy back in 1965," she says. "But I don't know if I could make it through Katrina by myself."

"That's why I'm here, Nana," you reply. "I have everything we need right here." You set your box on the kitchen table.

You stay up most of the night and through the morning listening to weather reports. Katrina makes landfall just after 6:00 a.m. The wind howls and the rain beats down on the roof.

Water pools in the street, but the flooding isn't serious. But you start moving things to the second floor, just to be safe. Katrina crosses the delta of the Mississippi River and then moves across Lake Borgne. The winds pick up as the storm's center passes the city and nears the Mississippi border northeast of New Orleans. Katrina's counterclockwise spinning winds whip across Lake Pontchartrain. They push up a huge storm surge through the canals that normally drain into the large lake.

Many roads near Lake Pontchartrain were completely under water.

Turn the page.

Around 7:00 a.m. the levee at the London Avenue Canal, near the Mirabeau Avenue Bridge, is breached. Floodwaters rush into the city. About two hours later the levee along the 17th Street Canal, just south of the Metairie-Hammond Bridge, gives way.

You look out the window. To your horror, water is pouring through the breach and into the neighborhood. It slams into Nana's house. You are shoved against a wall as the house is lifted off its foundation and spins around. Then the walls collapse.

Investigators found the 17th Street Canal failed after water rose only halfway up the floodwall, causing massive flooding.

"Help me!" Nana cries. But her shouts are quickly muffled by the water and debris that smothers you.

As the water bursts through the breach in the 17th Street Canal, it fills the houses near the levee. When rescue workers get to Nana's house days later, they find your bodies buried beneath a pile of debris.

THE END

To follow another path, turn to page 11.
To read the conclusion, turn to page 101.

Even though your store is only a one-story cement building, you choose to stay there. It is farther from Lake Pontchartrain and the drainage canals than your grandmother's house. It's a sturdier building than your grandma's wooden house and has a tiny attic that you can escape to if the water rises. You drive over to your grandmother's.

"Are we leaving town?" she asks.

"No, Nana," you reply as you load her things into your car. "We're going to ride out the storm at my store."

You let people come into the store throughout the night to buy supplies. They are wet and windblown. But they are thankful for the few things you have left.

You stay up most of Sunday night listening to weather reports. Katrina makes landfall just after 6:00 a.m. Monday. The wind howls and the rain pours. As the eye of the storm passes to the east of New Orleans, there's some water in the streets. But overall, it doesn't seem bad. There is flooding in St. Bernard Parish and the Lower Ninth Ward. But it sounds as if most of the city has been spared.

"How's it look outside?" Nana asks.

"The wind seems to be picking up," you reply, a little worried.

As Katrina crosses Lake Borgne, its counterclockwise winds whip back across Lake Pontchartrain. They push the huge storm surge into the canals that normally drain water from the city into the lake.

Turn the page.

A convenience store with no roof
stayed open to help survivors after
Hurricane Katrina.

The London Avenue Canal, near the Mirabeau Avenue Bridge, is breached. Then the levee along the 17th Street Canal, just south of the lake, gives way. The western portion of Orleans Parish floods.

Suddenly water is rushing into your store. You grab an ax.

"Come on, Nana, let's get to the attic!" you yell.

"Don't forget my oxygen tank!" she shouts as you pull her upstairs.

The water creeps up the stairs behind you. You quickly chop a hole in the roof, just to be safe. You're relieved that the water stops before it covers the top step.

61

The storm reaches Mississippi and heads north. Then the temperatures rise. The heat is sweltering inside the attic. The small thermometer on the wall reads 105 degrees.

Turn the page.

You help Nana and her oxygen tank onto the roof. You scramble up after her.

As you look around, you are surprised to see that your neighborhood has become a lake. Rooftops dot its surface. You aren't the only ones stranded by the floodwaters. Others peek out of second-story windows or holes chopped in roofs. In the coming days, the water will creep through the city, flooding nearly 80 percent of New Orleans.

Many survivors climbed onto their roofs to wait for rescue.

You worry if you will have enough food and water, and how long Nana's oxygen will last. As the hours pass, you make her take regular sips of water. You drink some too, but you want to save most of it for her. You're almost relieved when night falls, because the air cools a bit. But you know that means you'll be spending the night stranded on the roof. You wrap a blanket around Nana and do your best to keep her comfortable.

The next morning the sun dawns bright and hot. You're even more worried about Nana. In the sweltering heat, her breathing is raspy and labored.

63

Late that morning you hear a whirring noise above you. It's a Coast Guard rescue helicopter!

Turn the page.

The U.S. Coast Guard used helicopters to rescue thousands of survivors stranded on rooftops.

You wave frantically and point to your grandmother.

"She needs help!" you shout.

A rescuer rappels from the helicopter to the roof. The helicopter crew then lowers a basket. You and the rescuer strap Nana in it. Moments later the crew lowers a harness for you. You and Nana are just two of the 50,000 people pulled from homes and other buildings after the storm.

The helicopter takes you both to a Coast Guard station. A medic tends to Nana while a volunteer hands you a bottle of water. You know it will probably be months before you can reopen your store—if ever. But for now, you're just thankful that you're both alive.

THE END

To follow another path, turn to page 11.
To read the conclusion, turn to page 101.

You are worried that if you wait for gas, the station might run out, and you will be stuck in the city as the storm hits. So you drive onto Interstate 10 and head west, out of town. But you are one of more than 1 million people evacuating the area. Traffic is thick.

You barely make it out of your neighborhood before your car begins to stall. You are out of gas.

You steer the car over to the shoulder of the road and sit there as cars slowly inch forward in the highway lanes. You know you can't stay here with the hurricane on its way. You decide to get out and walk home. Maybe you can find a place to wait out the worst of the storm.

Strong winds and flying debris made driving very dangerous during the storm.

As you get out of your car, powerful winds swirl about. You can barely stay on your feet because of the gusts.

Suddenly you hear a metallic screech. You look up into the rain. Just ahead of you, the wind tears a highway sign from its post. As the metal sign comes whirring toward you, you scream. You realize your mistake too late. Flying debris can be deadly during a hurricane.

THE END

To follow another path, turn to page 11.
To read the conclusion, turn to page 101.

You sigh and tell Jenny she's right. You can't stop worrying about Nana and Lori, though. It's several days before you hear from Lori. She says she and Nana traveled by bus to the Astrodome in Houston, Texas. The Sunday after the storm, you drive to Houston to get them. You take them to Jenny's house in Lafayette.

You are all safe. But it takes more than a week for the levee breaches to be filled. And it is many days before the water filling your neighborhood is pumped out. Months pass before power and water services are restored. But you are determined to return. In the coming months, your store will be a lifeline for your neighbors as they struggle to rebuild.

THE END

To follow another path, turn to page 11.
To read the conclusion, turn to page 101.

It isn't safe to return to New Orleans right now, but you have to find your family. You get in your car and start driving east on Interstate 10.

As you enter the city, you see people standing on overpasses and bridges. They wave their arms and shout, "Help us!" as you drive past. But you don't dare stop.

Just then you notice steam coming from under your car's hood. You know what that means—the engine has overheated. You have no choice but to pull over to the right side of the highway. As you get out of your steaming car, a man and a woman walk over to you.

69

Turn the page.

The man shakes his head in disbelief. "What are you doing?" he asks. "We're doing anything we can to get out of this mess of a city, and you're trying to get back in?"

"My sister and grandma are at the Superdome," you tell him. "I'm scared something bad has happened to them."

"We came from the Superdome," the woman says. "It's a mess there for sure. We're waiting for someone to get us out of the city."

The highway into downtown New Orleans was deserted after people evacuated the city.

You wait with the couple, Miguel and Debbie, for several hours before buses show up to take you to the Astrodome in Houston, Texas. By Saturday afternoon both the Superdome and the Convention Center have been evacuated. You reunite with Lori and Nana at the Astrodome, but you don't know what you'll do next. You've lost your home, your business, and your car. Maybe you'll stay in Texas and try to start over.

THE END

To follow another path, turn to page 11.
To read the conclusion, turn to page 101.

Highways and bridges were swept away when Hurricane Katrina hit Mississippi on August 29, 2005.

CHAPTER 4

Battling in Biloxi

You live in Biloxi, Mississippi, a city of more than 50,000. It sits at the end of a peninsula, so it's surrounded by water. The Gulf of Mexico runs along Biloxi's southern edge, while Back Bay of Biloxi is north of the city. With beaches along the Gulf and floating casinos dotting the coast, it is a popular vacation spot.

You're a firefighter at a station on the east end of the city. You've listened to reports of Hurricane Katrina as it ripped across Florida and entered the Gulf of Mexico.

73

Turn the page.

When Governor Haley Barbour declares a state of emergency for Mississippi, your station is put on high alert.

You weren't born when Hurricane Camille struck Mississippi in 1969, but you have heard stories of the powerful category 5 hurricane. More than 250 people died, and the storm caused more than $1 billion in damages.

The National Oceanic and Atmospheric Administration (NOAA) records waves 30 feet high off Alabama's coast. The floodwalls along the county's major beaches are less than half that height.

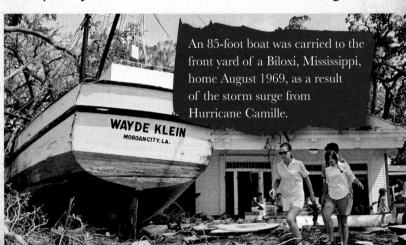

An 85-foot boat was carried to the front yard of a Biloxi, Mississippi, home August 1969, as a result of the storm surge from Hurricane Camille.

Mayor A. J. Holloway of Biloxi orders all casinos to close within 48 hours of Katrina's predicted landfall. By Sunday, August 28, everyone is ordered out of the hotels along the coast.

Local officials order a mandatory evacuation of the area. You even hear the mayor on the radio pleading with residents to leave. "Hurricane Katrina is a killer storm …"

Most people listen to him. But not everyone. Some people simply can't afford a tank of gas or the cost of a few nights in a hotel. Others feel they don't need to leave. Their houses are higher than where Hurricane Camille's storm surge reached. During that storm water never even made it to your station.

Turn the page.

Your parents, brother, and sister are packing up their things and leaving the city. They plan on staying with your aunt and uncle in McComb. They think that town is far enough north of Katrina's projected path to escape the worst of the storm. On Sunday your boss, Captain Maria Stevens, gives you a half-day off to settle things at home.

To help your family, go to page **77.**
To stay at the station, turn to page **79.**

You head home to help your family pack their car. McComb is just a little more than two hours' drive from Biloxi. You decide to pack your truck with some of your family's belongings and drive to your aunt and uncle's house. You want to be back in Biloxi before late afternoon.

On a typical day, you would just follow Interstate 10 west to Interstate 55 and head north. But on Sunday morning, Mayor Ray Nagin of New Orleans orders a mandatory evacuation of the city.

Signs mark hurricane evacuation routes. Many highways became one-way only to help people evacuate.

Turn the page.

People have already been streaming out of the city, but now there is more traffic on the major highways. Most of the lanes are being used for outgoing traffic. You and your dad decide to take back roads. The trip takes you nearly twice as long as normal. You don't arrive until late Sunday afternoon.

You unpack and see that your family gets settled inside. "What are you going to do?" Dad asks. "The weather's getting rough. You might be better off staying with us."

You worry about the dangers of driving back to Biloxi. As Mayor Holloway said, Katrina is a killer storm.

"Won't your department need you?" your sister, Katie, asks.

To return to Biloxi, turn to page **82**.
To stay with your family, turn to page **87**.

You call your family. "Mom, I won't be able to help you pack," you say. "We have too much going on at the station."

"I understand," she says. "We'll be fine. Just take care of yourself."

Then you start preparing the station. Even though you don't expect floodwaters to reach it, you board the windows. You gather extra supplies, such as blankets, canned food, and water. You encourage anyone you see outside to leave the city.

"Remember what the mayor said," you shout. "Katrina is a killer storm."

Some say they are leaving. Others just shrug their shoulders like they don't care.

Turn the page.

Boats washed up on shore when Hurricane Katrina hit the Gulf Coast.

You and six other firefighters, along with Captain Stevens, huddle by a radio to listen to the weather reports on Monday, August 29. Katrina makes landfall in Louisiana around 6:00 a.m.

As the storm moves toward Mississippi, you and the other firefighters start to worry. The state is on the east side of the storm. With its winds circling counterclockwise over the Gulf, the brunt of the storm is hitting Mississippi's coast.

It's raining and the winds are picking up. As the minutes pass, you hear reports of flooding from Waveland and Bay St. Louis. Highway 90 has been washed out in places. Then you hear of flooding farther inland, along Interstate 10. The water levels are rising dangerously high.

"This is sounding worse than Camille," Captain Stevens says. "I'm not sure if we should stay here or head over to the main station on Porter Avenue."

"If we leave, we'd better do it now," your fellow firefighter Rachel says. "The storm surge is already beating on Biloxi's beaches."

"But what if people need us here?" Matt, another firefighter, asks.

To stay at the station, turn to page **91**.
To leave the station, turn to page **96**.

"I think my department will need me," you tell Katie. Traffic is thick as you head back to Biloxi on Highway 98 East. But your car is one of just a few headed in the direction of the storm. You stay well north of the worst of the storm, as you turn south on Highway 13 at Columbia. That road takes you to Highway 49 South, which connects to Interstate 10.

You listen to the weather reports. Katrina makes landfall in Louisiana just after 6:00 a.m. Then it moves over Lake Borgne toward the Louisiana-Mississippi border. Mississippi is on the east side of the storm, which is its strong side. With winds whipping counterclockwise over the Gulf, Katrina sends a 20-foot storm surge bearing down on Biloxi.

It is sometime after 7:00 a.m. when you finally get onto Interstate 10. You try to hurry, but between the heavy rain and gusting winds, you can't even drive the speed limit.

To your amazement, water is starting to creep onto the highway, even though you are about nine miles inland. As you drive over the Highway 605 overpass, you notice the Biloxi River has flooded its banks. Wind-blown water covers the bridge over the river.

Roads leading toward the areas in Katrina's path were empty as people evacuate.

Turn the page.

In front of you, you see a car stuck in the water. It must have stalled before it could get over the bridge. The water has risen nearly up to its windows. Through the rain, you can't see if there is anyone inside.

You jump out of your truck. You run down the overpass and slog through waist-deep water to get to the car. Once there, you are horrified to see two people, a man and a woman, in the front seats. A little boy is strapped into a car seat in back. Both adults are struggling to push their doors open, but the pressure of the rising water is too strong.

You rap on the driver-side window, and yell, "Roll down your window!"

The man rolls down the window. "Save my son!" he yells. He reaches back to unbuckle the boy. You lean into the car, grab the child, and pull him out.

"Crawl out the windows!" you yell to the parents.

You carry the boy in your arms as you all head back up the overpass and get into your truck. You learn that the parents' names are Sarah and Dave, and the boy is Trevor. Rain beats down on your windows and wind rocks the truck, but you and the family are safe inside.

Turn the page.

Floodwaters covered Highway 90 in Gulfport, Mississippi.

In front of you, you watch the water creep over the roof of the car until it is completely submerged.

"We're lucky you came along," Sarah says.

While you weren't able to make it back to your fire station, you can at least say you played an important role during the storm. You rescued three people from drowning.

THE END

To follow another path, turn to page 11.
To read the conclusion, turn to page 101.

You decide that you don't have time to make it back to Biloxi before the storm, not with the traffic pouring out of New Orleans. Plus, Mayor Holloway's words of warning echo through your thoughts. "You're probably right, Dad," you say.

"Then come on back inside," your dad says. "Uncle Ralph will fry some catfish for us."

You are far enough to the north and west of Katrina's path that all you suffer are some heavy rains and gusting winds. The power goes out, but the damage to Uncle Ralph and Aunt Lucy's house and nearby trees is minor.

Turn the page.

Then you start hearing reports of flooding from New Orleans to Biloxi. Hundreds die and hundreds of thousands of homes are destroyed.

You wonder how your fellow firefighters are weathering the storm. You're feeling as if you should have made more effort to get back to your job.

When you finally make it back to your fire station, Captain Stevens greets you.

In Mississippi, 238 people lost their lives as a result of Hurricane Katrina.

"You're on leave without pay until the fire chief schedules a hearing on whether you should be allowed to come back to work," Captain Stevens says.

Upset, you return home. You're relieved to see your house escaped with little damage. Even though you can't go back to your job, you can at least volunteer to help the storm victims.

Cleanup takes months, and the fire chief doesn't have time to listen to your case. Meanwhile, your savings run out. You decide to quit and find another job to pay your bills. You're sorry that your decision to stay in McComb caused you to lose the job you loved.

THE END

To follow another path, turn to page 11.
To read the conclusion, turn to page 101.

Many people who stayed in Mississippi were forced out of their houses by floodwaters.

You decide to stay at the station. While the water is getting close, it has never reached this far in earlier storms. Plus, you know that not everyone has left the city. People in your neighborhood might need help.

Katrina nears the border of Louisiana and Mississippi as a powerful category 3 hurricane. Its winds swirl at more than 120 miles per hour. Water is lapping at the fire station and leaking under the door. Over the noise of the storm, you hear someone pounding on the front door.

"Help! Help! Let us in!"

Nearly 20 local residents, wet and ragged, are seeking shelter. Floodwaters have chased them from their homes.

Turn the page.

But the floodwaters don't stop there. They keep rising. Inside, you and the other firefighters help the people onto the station's trucks. The water rises to your waist and then your chest. It doesn't stop rising until it is up to your neck.

With all the people on the trucks, there's no room for you. You cling to a truck's side. You tread water. You do everything you can to keep your head above the water. You are just thankful that you are inside the station. Outside, the wind and white-capped waves are beating at the brick walls. You don't know if you could keep yourself safe out in the storm, let alone 20 civilians.

It feels like hours before the water starts to subside and you can set your feet on solid ground. Once the storm has passed and you dare step outside, you see the destruction Katrina caused. Homes are destroyed. Debris is strewn everywhere.

Rachel suggests you head down to check out the Gulf Coast. You join her and Matt in your truck. The destruction is just as bad there.

Many local residents and businesses along Biloxi's beach front lost everything because of the storm.

Turn the page.

"Hey, look at that," Rachel says. She points to the Biloxi Lighthouse. "I can't believe it's still standing."

"Looks like it took a bit of a beating, though," you reply.

The lighthouse was built in 1848, but weathered the storm better than many of the newer buildings along the coast. In the following weeks, months, and years, Biloxi struggles to rebuild. But every time you see the lighthouse, you feel that it's all worthwhile. This symbol of hope helps you keep going.

THE END

To follow another path, turn to page 11.
To read the conclusion, turn to page 101.

The Biloxi Lighthouse is a popular landmark and became a symbol of strength for the city after Katrina.

95

As more reports come in, you hear of waves ripping some of the floating casinos from their moorings and throwing them onto shore. Water is flowing up on all sides of the peninsula. You can even see it creeping toward your fire station. You decide to leave.

You lock up the station. The eight firefighters in your station board two trucks and head for the main station on Porter Avenue.

The Palace Casino in Biloxi was partially submerged and severely damaged by Hurricane Katrina.

You drive slowly through pouring rain. The streets are deserted and the skies black.

The station's chief is surprised to see you. "Why are you here?" he asks. "Is your station flooded out?"

"Water was creeping up on it," you say. "We decided to leave before it flooded."

"I just hope no one in your neighborhood needs help," he replies. "But since you're here, we could use you."

Throughout the storm, you help any displaced people that come your way. You give them warm blankets and help them out of the weather.

97

Turn the page.

Hurricane Katrina destroyed structures along highways, including Highway 90 in Biloxi.

There's no flooding at the Porter Avenue station. But looking out a second-story window toward the Gulf, you see water covers Highway 90, which is only a couple of blocks away. The storm even lifted one of the casinos onto the highway.

After the storm passes, you and Matt head back to your station. Trees are down, thousands of homes destroyed, and garbage from the storm surge is everywhere.

Then you see a sad sight. The bodies of two people are near the station's front door. They join the more than 50 people who drowned in Biloxi during the storm.

"They must have come here looking for shelter," Matt says.

You feel horrible. If you had not left the station, you might have been able to help them.

THE END

To follow another path, turn to page 11.
To read the conclusion, turn to page 101.

Residents and city officials pledged to rebuild after more than 1 million people were displaced by Hurricane Katrina.

I AM HOME! I WILL REBUILD! I AM NEW ORLEANS!

CHAPTER 5

The Most Destructive U.S. Storm

Of New Orleans' nearly 500,000 residents, about 100,000 were left in the city when Hurricane Katrina hit. They had various reasons for staying, just like the people who stayed along Mississippi's Gulf Coast. Many didn't have a way out of the city or couldn't afford to leave. Others wanted to protect their belongings. Some even thought they could ride out the storm like they had during past hurricanes.

After the storm the number of people killed was highly exaggerated, with some saying more than 10,000 died. To date, that number is believed to be about 1,800.

101

Turn the page.

Most of the deaths occurred in Louisiana, with 238 in Mississippi. About half died from drowning or injuries from flying debris. Others died of heat stroke, dehydration, or from lack of needed medical care for health problems.

In the Superdome there were rumors of several murders. Of the six people believed to have died there, four deaths were from natural causes, one was a drug overdose, and one was a suicide. Four people died at the Convention Center. One appeared to have been stabbed, while the other three died of natural causes.

While Katrina wasn't the deadliest hurricane in U.S. history, it can be argued that it was the most destructive. Estimated damages along the Gulf Coast have risen to more than $135 billion.

Hundreds of thousands of houses were destroyed and many more were damaged. It took months to restore power and water to the hardest-hit areas. Thousands of businesses were hurt by the storm. In the following months, gas prices spiked across the nation because of the halt in production that Katrina caused.

There are many reasons why Hurricane Katrina caused so much damage. Several studies have shown that the levees protecting New Orleans were poorly designed and built.

At first people thought the water entering the city was from the storm surge overtopping the levees. It was learned that in many cases, the levees simply gave way because of design and construction flaws.

Turn the page.

Ivor van Heerden, PhD, argues that part of the problem is development around the city. Van Heerden was the deputy director of the Louisiana State University Hurricane Center. Much of the wetlands along the Mississippi Delta have been dredged to create canals for commercial shipping and oil and gas exploration. Other wetlands were drained to create more land for the city to expand. As levees prevent the Mississippi River from overflowing its banks, wetlands aren't replenished by sediment from the river.

Wetlands work as a sponge during a storm. As a storm surge flows through them, the wetlands absorb water, limiting the storm's force as it surges inland. About 1,800 square miles of wetlands have been lost along Louisiana's coast since 1930. Louisiana is putting plans in place to restore the wetlands and this natural storm protection.

People along the Gulf Coast are proud to have mostly recovered. Homes have been rebuilt and businesses are booming. Many changes have been made to prevent another disaster. The levee system has been made stronger. A new 1.8-mile barrier across Lake Borgne now provides more protection from storm surges. When storms threaten, people who need help evacuating are provided bus transportation to safe shelters elsewhere in Louisiana.

Tourists are again flocking to New Orleans for its delicious food and famous jazz music. The beaches along Mississippi's coast are filled with people seeking sun and good fishing. But there are still reminders, from abandoned homes to lost heirlooms, of Hurricane Katrina's devastation. It will forever be a lesson to those living along the Gulf Coast of nature's destructive force.

TIMELINE

2005

Wednesday, August 24—Weather satellites detect a tropical storm in the Bahamas; the National Hurricane Center names the storm Katrina.

Thursday, August 25—A category 1 hurricane, Katrina crosses the southern tip of Florida; it causes 14 deaths and more than $500 million in damages.

Friday, August 26—Katrina reaches the Gulf of Mexico and becomes a category 2 hurricane.

Saturday, August 27—Katrina reaches category 3; President George W. Bush declares a federal state of emergency for Louisiana; Mayor A. J. Holloway orders a mandatory evacuation of Biloxi, Mississippi.

Sunday, August 28—Katrina becomes a category 5 hurricane, with winds of more than 155 miles per hour; Mayor Ray Nagin orders a mandatory evacuation of New Orleans.

Monday, August 29

5:02 a.m.—The Superdome, where many people in New Orleans have taken shelter, loses power.

6:10 a.m.—Katrina makes landfall in New Orleans as a category 3 hurricane.

4:00 a.m., 7:00–8:00 a.m.—Breaches occur along the Industrial Canal floodwall in the Lower Ninth Ward.

7:00 a.m.—London Avenue Canal levee is breached.

9:00 a.m.—17th Street Canal levee is breached.

9:45 a.m.—After crossing Lake Borgne, Katrina comes ashore along the border between Louisiana and Mississippi; as levees fail in New Orleans, Biloxi suffers major flooding.

10:00 p.m.—Katrina is downgraded to a tropical storm.

Tuesday, August 30—While the storm has moved on, floodwaters continue to pour into New Orleans.

Thursday, September 1—FEMA buses begin to take people from the Superdome to other shelters outside the state.

Friday, September 2—U.S. Army National Guard soldiers and supply trucks bring food and water to people at the Superdome and Convention Center.

Saturday, September 3—The last FEMA bus leaves the Superdome at 5:47 p.m.

2006

September 25—The repaired Superdome reopens.

OTHER PATHS TO EXPLORE

In this book you've learned how people struggled to survive during a devastating storm. These stories are based on the hardships of people who chose not to evacuate. But the majority of people did leave as Katrina approached.

Perspectives on history are as varied as the people who lived it. Seeing history from many points of view is an important part of understanding it. Here are ideas for other points of view to explore.

Many people evacuated their homes before Hurricane Katrina struck. What was it like for them being away from their homes for weeks and months? What did they find upon returning? (Common Core: Key Ideas and Details)

Government organizations established several rescue teams to help find victims of the storm. Describe some of these rescues. Look at the text to find the steps the rescuers took. (Common Core: Craft and Structure)

What are some of the reasons Hurricane Katrina was so destructive to New Orleans? What are some solutions being put in place to prevent another disaster? Which of these solutions do you think might be most effective? Explain why you think so. (Common Core: Integration of Knowledge and Ideas)

READ MORE

Benoit, Peter. *Hurricane Katrina.* New York: Children's Press, 2012.

Furgang, Kathy. *Everything Weather.* Washington, D.C.: National Geographic, 2012.

Tarshis, Lauren. *I Survived Hurricane Katrina, 2005.* New York: Scholastic, 2011.

Palser, Barb. *Hurricane Katrina: Aftermath of Disaster.* Minneapolis: Compass Point Books, 2007

INTERNET SITES

Use FactHound to find Internet sites related to this book. All of the sites on FactHound have been researched by our staff.

Here's all you do:

Visit *www.facthound.com*

Type in this code: 9781476541891

GLOSSARY

assault (uh-SAWLT)—to attack someone or something

canal (kuh-NAL)—a channel that is dug to connect bodies of water

debris (duh-BREE)—the scattered pieces of something that has been broken or damaged

delta (DEL-tuh)—the triangle-shaped area where a river deposits mud, sand, and pebbles

evacuate (i-VAK-yoo-ate)—to leave an area because of the danger there

landfall (LAND-fawl)—the act of reaching land

levee (LEV-ee)—a bank built up along a river or canal to prevent flooding

mandatory (MAN-duh-tor-ee)—something that is required or commanded by law

parish (PA-rish)—a Louisiana county

peninsula (puh-NIN-suh-luh)—a narrow strip of land with water on three sides

storm surge (STORM SURJ)—a huge wave of water pushed ashore by a hurricane

ward (WAHRD)—a district of New Orleans

BIBLIOGRAPHY

Brinkley, Douglas. *The Great Deluge: Hurricane Katrina, New Orleans, and the Mississippi Gulf Coast.* New York: Morrow, 2006.

Editors of Time Magazine. *Hurricane Katrina: The Storm That Changed America.* New York: Time Books, 2005.

Greater New Orleans Community Data Center: Lower Ninth Ward Statistical Area. 31 Oct. 2013. http://gnocdc.org/NeighborhoodData/8/LowerNinthWard/index.html

Horne, Jed. *Breach of Faith: Hurricane Katrina and the Near Death of a Great American City.* New York: Random House, 2008.

Hurricane Katrina. History.com. 31 Oct. 2013. http://www.history.com/topics/hurricane-katrina

Hurricane Katrina. National Geographic. 31 Oct. 2013. http://www.nationalgeographic.com/topics/hurricane-katrina

Hurricane Katrina Timeline. 31 Oct. 2013. http://uspolitics.about.com/library/bl_katrina_timeline.htm

Smith, James Patterson. *Hurricane Katrina: The Mississippi Story.* Jackson: University Press of Mississippi, 2012.

Teen Survivors of Hurricane Katrina. PBS NewsHour Extra. 31 Oct. 2013. http://www.pbs.org/newshour/extra/features/july-dec05/survivors_9-12.html

The Man Who Predicted Katrina. NOVA. 31 Oct. 2013. http://www.pbs.org/wgbh/nova/earth/predicting-katrina.html

INDEX